BOOKS AND THE
Founding Fathers

GEORGE H. NASH

ISBN 1-884532-91-8

Book Design by Scott Stortz

Printed in USA

Published by
Butler Books
P.O. Box 7311
Louisville, KY 40207
(502) 897-9393
Fax (502) 897-9797

www.butlerbooks.com

Acknowledgments

This essay is a revision of a lecture first delivered in 1987 in Washington, D. C., at the headquarters of the National Society of the Daughters of the American Revolution. The lecture was subsequently published by the Center for the Book at the Library of Congress, in the Center's Viewpoint series. I am grateful to the Center's director, John Y. Cole, both for arranging publication of the original lecture and for encouraging me to reproduce it here, in somewhat altered form, when the opportunity arose.

For that opportunity I am grateful to the McConnell Center at the University of Louisville and its director, Gary L. Gregg. It was Dr. Gregg who invited me to update and amplify the lecture and to include with it a bibliographical essay, first for presentation at the University in celebration of Constitution Day 2006, and then for distribution in book form. It is a pleasure to circulate my reflections on the Founding Fathers to a new generation of readers under the auspices of the McConnell Center.

I thank Emma Kuipers for once again providing efficient typing and computer support, as she has done on many occasions for me in the last decade.

Finally, I salute my subjects, the Founding Fathers, whose devotion to liberty and learning earned them the gratitude of posterity that they sought. It is always rewarding to pay them a visit.

– George H. Nash

Table of Contents

Introduction

The books that we read help inform our minds about the facts of the world and form our imaginations as to the many possibilities in human affairs. The books that we don't read (but should) leave our minds uninformed and our imaginations unshaped. Our Founding Fathers understood well the importance of books and took them very seriously. They were shaped by a curriculum and a culture that valued the great books of the western canon. Their knowledge of Greek philosophy, Roman law, Judeo-Christian sacred texts and apologetics, the works of the Scottish Enlightenment, and English history and literature all formed their understanding of the world and fueled their imaginative enterprise of founding a new nation—a *novus ordo seclorum.*

To the extent that we no longer read the books that informed our founders, we are distanced from them and their project. To the extent we are distanced from their project, we are separated from the American experiment of which we are merely the current manifestation.

Would John Adams have been who he was and done all that he did during our revolution if he had not paced the floors of his room at night declaiming Cicero? Would Thomas Jefferson have been able to pen the soaring language of our Declaration of Independence had he not spent evenings alone with the plays of Shakespeare and the orations of Demosthenes? Would George Washington have persevered through the long and difficult revolution, had he not spent evenings contemplating the republican virtue of Cato, the stoic statesman of Rome who resisted Caesar until his very last breath? Would Washington have been able to give us the great gift of his resignation of power after the revolution was won, had he not read of the powerful example of Cincinnatus?

Thomas Jefferson once said, "I cannot live without books." More literally, it can be said that America could not have lived without books, and particularly those books discussed in George H. Nash's essay that follows. As you read this little book, we hope you reflect on your own education and the books that are forming (or not forming) who you are and what you will become. Not only your own future, but the future of America may well depend on the reading choices you and your generation make today.

Gary L. Gregg II, Ph.D.
Mitch McConnell Chair in Leadership
University of Louisville

Malana S. Salyer
Civics Education Coordinator
McConnell Center, University of Louisville

"I cannot live without books."

Thomas Jefferson to John Adams
1815

BOOKS AND THE Founding Fathers

Books and the Founding Fathers

I wonder how many people know the origin of the phrase the "Founding Fathers." It seems that the person who coined this term was Warren Harding, the President of the United States in the early 1920s. In a speech on George Washington's birthday in 1918, Harding, at that time a senator from Ohio, mentioned what he called "the fountains of wisdom inherited from the founding fathers of the republic." Three years later, in his inaugural address as President, Harding declared: "I must utter my belief in the divine inspiration of the founding fathers."

Although no one today would place Harding himself in the intellectual company of the framers of our Constitution, few Americans would contest the sentiments that prompted his felicitous phrasemaking. Indeed, the impulse to honor the founders of our republic and learn more about them has intensified in our own time. In the past generation, as we have celebrated the bicentennial first of our independence and then of the Constitution and Bill of Rights that secured it, we have been treated to a veritable feast of books assessing the achievement of the revolutionary generation. Every year new volumes appear, narrating, interpreting, and documenting the process by which the Founders and their contemporaries created a regime of ordered liberty unique in all history. In just the past five years, monumental biographies of Benjamin Franklin, John Adams, and Alexander Hamilton have made the best seller lists, along with new studies of George Washington and Thomas Jefferson.

---

1 By "Founding Fathers" I refer not just to the fifty-five men who convened in Philadelphia in 1787 but to their leading contemporaries—such as John Adams, Thomas Jefferson, John Jay, and Patrick Henry—who did not attend but who obviously shaped the founding era.

In the essay that follows, I shall not tread directly over this familiar ground. Instead, I propose to explore a theme that has received less attention. I wish to examine some of the ways that the written word—specifically, books and libraries—molded the remarkable elite that made and preserved the American Revolution.

The first observation that comes forcibly to mind is that the great majority of the Founding Fathers[1] were, in fact, readers. Surveying the records of the Constitutional Convention of 1787, of the state ratifying conventions that followed, and the political/philosophical tracts produced by Federalists and Anti-Federalists alike, one is struck repeatedly by the debaters' invocation of history, particularly that of ancient Rome and post-Elizabethan Britain. With seeming ease and obvious confidence that their audiences would understand them, they referred to past episodes and personages, thereby exhibiting a form of knowledge derived, in the last analysis, from books. This impression is reinforced by a perusal of the political pamphlet literature that flourished in astonishing profusion in America between 1763 and the 1790s—pamphlets often replete with Latin quotations as well as references to ancient and modern authors. Our impression grows even stronger when we sample the correspondence of the Founding Fathers—most notably, the incomparable letters exchanged between Thomas Jefferson and John Adams in their old age. "[R]eading is my delight," wrote Jefferson to Adams late in life. In letter after scintillating letter, the two men exchanged views on books that they had been reading.

The Founding Fathers' acquaintance with the written word was not confined to works in the English language. For many of them, Greek and Latin were virtually second tongues. Jefferson was fluent in French and Spanish as well, and he was not the only one with such linguistic ability—Benjamin Franklin was another. John Adams owned books in eight languages and read Cervantes, Voltaire, and Rousseau in the original. All in all, late eighteenth century America was a demonstrably literate civilization; its literacy rate, in fact, was probably the highest in the world. And at its apex was a singular array of individuals who were men of learning as well as men of power.

What did these busy lawyers, merchants, agribusinessmen, and politicians actually read? From their surviving correspondence and other writings, a clear, composite picture quickly emerges. First, the men of the revolutionary generation were, for the most part, steeped in what are known as the classics. Herodotus, Thucydides, Plutarch, Tacitus, Sallust, and Cicero—from these and other famous men of letters, the framers of the Constitution obtained their knowledge of ancient history. History, in fact, was of consuming interest to the Founders; it was not just something they had to study in school. Nor was its subject matter confined to far-off Greece and Rome. The history of modern Great Britain—and particularly its generations-long internal struggles for liberty—had, for the catalysts of our independence, an endless appeal. Not surprisingly, many of them were strongly attracted to the so-called Whig theory of history, propounded by (among others) the British writer and political activist Catherine Macaulay, whose eight-volume *History of England from the Accession of James I to That of the Brunswick Line* (1763-1783) achieved great popularity on this side of the Atlantic. When Mrs. Macaulay, who sympathized with the American cause, visited the United States in 1785, she was entertained by George Washington himself at Mount Vernon.

Ranking with history as a focus of the Founders' reading interests was what we today call political philosophy. Their favorite sources were extraordinarily varied: from Aristotle among the ancients to their Scottish contemporary, David Hume ("The Judicious Hume," Alexander Hamilton once labeled him). Particularly prominent on the Founders' bookshelves was the outpouring of eighteenth century English libertarian or "Opposition" literature exemplified by Bolingbroke, James Burgh, and *Cato's Letters*, authored by John Trenchard and Thomas Gordon. Another exceedingly popular political theorist was John Locke, whose *Two Treatises of Government* achieved almost iconic status; Jefferson ranked Locke with Francis Bacon and Isaac Newton as the three greatest men who had ever lived. Also significant was the influence of the Scottish Enlightenment, particularly in the emerging field of political economy pioneered by Sir James Steuart and Adam Smith, author of *The Wealth of Nations* (1776). From France came Montesquieu's *Spirit of the Laws* (1748) and, a generation later, the writings of the physiocrats. From Switzerland came the natural law writings of Burlamaqui and Vattel.

This is not the place to appraise the relative impact of the streams of thought represented by these towering and extremely diverse thinkers. My point, rather, is that the leading political figures of late eighteenth-century America were generally, and often intimately, acquainted with the output of the greatest European minds of their day—and of the minds of the ancient western world. I repeat: the Founding Fathers (with few exceptions) were readers.

Not surprisingly, since so many of them by profession were lawyers, Sir William Blackstone's massive *Commentaries on the Laws of England* became a fixture of their personal libraries and a resource that they repeatedly cited in public debate. And although history, political philosophy, and law dominated their serious reading, these practical-minded statesmen were by no means unfamiliar with literature—or, as it was then often called, *belles lettres*. John Adams, for instance, owned complete sets of Homer, Plato, Horace, Ovid, and Marcus Aurelius—to mention a few of the classical authors most popular in his generation. The Bible and Shakespeare also formed part of the literary patrimony of the Founders. Even contemporary English poetry and fiction did not escape their attention. In his later years, Adams, for one, frankly enjoyed what he called "romances." In this, however, the founders of our country were not unanimous. The somewhat didactic Jefferson told a friend in 1818 that the novels of his day were a "mass of trash"—"poison [that] infects the mind" and becomes "a great obstacle to good education." Fiction should have moral utility, he argued. "Nothing of mere amusement," he declared, "should lumber a public library."

Two factors above all placed an ineffaceable stamp on the reading habits of the American revolutionaries. The first was the prevailing mode of their education: rigorous, classical, and thoroughly book-oriented. As early as the ages of eight or nine, either in schools or the custody of private tutors, colonial boys entered into concentrated study of Greek and Latin. This was no casual affectation; demonstrated proficiency in these languages was a prerequisite to entrance into college (and more than half of the fifty-five men who convened in Philadelphia in 1787 attended college). Upon entering college, which American males in those days customarily did in their early to mid-teens, they could expect to encounter most of the authors whom I have previously mentioned.

Consider, for example, the higher education of William Paterson, who later represented New Jersey at the Constitutional Convention. After passing entrance examinations in Latin and Greek, he enrolled in the College of New Jersey (now Princeton University) in 1759, at the age of fourteen. For the next four years he immersed himself in ancient history and literature, as well as such English authors as Shakespeare, Milton, Swift, and Pope. Here also—like James Madison, who matriculated after him—young Paterson took the required senior course in moral philosophy, a crucial transmission belt for the ideas that young men absorbed about human conduct. It was, in part, through Princeton's curriculum that the writings of such eminent Scottish social theorists as Adam Smith, Adam Ferguson, and Thomas Reid entered American intellectual and political life.

Even legal education was not exempt from this relentlessly bookish approach to learning. Consider the course of study that Thomas Jefferson composed in 1767 (at age twenty-four) for a friend who was about to study to be a lawyer. Before his friend was to begin his course of legal studies, Jefferson counseled that he must "absolutely" learn Latin and French, and should become conversant with mathematics, astronomy, geography, and natural philosophy. Having laid this foundation, said Jefferson, his friend could properly embark on his quest.

This, however, was only the beginning. With characteristic thoroughness, Jefferson next prescribed a systematic outline of study for his friend, including every single book that the would-be lawyer should read. Before eight o'clock in the morning he should employ himself in what Jefferson called "Physical Studies," including agriculture, chemistry, anatomy, zoology, botany, ethics, "natural" religion, "sectarian" religion, and natural law. From eight until noon he should read Law. From twelve to one he should read politics, and during the afternoon, history. From dark until bedtime he should concentrate on *belles lettres* (notably Shakespeare), criticism, rhetoric, and oratory, particularly the orations of Demosthenes and Cicero. In other words, to obtain a satisfactory legal education, one should read books for as many as twelve hours a day—and only a third of that time should the books be about law!

If Jefferson's advice appears manifestly utopian to us, one suspects that it seemed much less so to his contemporaries. Only fourteen years before the future Sage of Monticello offered his formidable regimen to his young acquaintance, another American statesman-in-the-making, John Dickinson, sailed to London for four strenuous years of legal studies. Rising daily at 5:00 A.M., he would read for nearly eight hours, dine at four o'clock, and then retire early in the evening—all the while mingling his scrutiny of legal texts with such authors as Tacitus and Bacon. In 1757, his formal education complete, Dickinson returned to Pennsylvania and started a distinguished career culminating in the "miracle at Philadelphia."

This, then, was the first influence that made the Founding Fathers the kind of readers they were. In eighteenth century America, education was a serious enterprise, entailing disciplined exposure to the "great tradition" of classical and enlightened learning. The colonial educational system imbued in its ablest matriculants a lifelong practice of diligent, humanistic reading. Perhaps it is not so surprising that one of the Constitution's framers, Benjamin Franklin, was the inventor of bifocals!

The second factor that profoundly affected the Founders' reading was, of course, the political and social upheaval of which they were the architects and beneficiaries. The illustrious men whom we celebrate today were contemplative activists engaged in a daring endeavor to which they had solemnly pledged their lives, their fortunes, and their sacred honor. Under these circumstances, it is not so startling that they repeatedly consulted the experience of the past—as recorded in works of history, law, and political theory—both to make sense of their current tribulations and to guide them in their epic task of nation-building. In a letter to his wife in 1780, during the most dismal days of the American Revolution, John Adams explained why he read the genres of literature that he did:

> I MUST STUDY POLITICKS AND WAR THAT MY SONS MAY HAVE LIBERTY TO STUDY MATHEMATICKS AND PHILOSOPHY. MY SONS OUGHT TO STUDY MATHEMATICKS AND PHILOSOPHY, GEOGRAPHY, NATURAL HISTORY, NAVAL ARCHITECTURE, NAVIGATION, COMMERCE AND AGRICULTURE, IN ORDER TO GIVE THEIR CHILDREN A RIGHT TO STUDY PAINTING, POETRY, MUSICK, ARCHITECTURE, STATUARY, TAPESTRY AND PORCELAIN.

For Adams, the kind of reading one permitted oneself in life was directly related to political concerns. The right to read books in the arts had to be earned.

The Founding Fathers' interest in books as a means of understanding "politics and war" had another, less conservative dimension. Like many European men of learning in that age known as the Enlightenment, the Americans who met in Philadelphia in 1787 believed that human nature was both universal and immutable, and that through the comparative study of past civilizations, they could adduce the fundamental principles of human behavior. In other words, history—particularly the history of ancient republics—could yield pertinent lessons for men embroiled in fashioning the unprecedented: a self-governing republic on a continental scale. In short, by careful historical research one could hope to gain an understanding of what Alexander Hamilton, in *Federalist* No. 9, unabashedly called the "science of politics." It was part of the Founders' faith that the "science of politics" had advanced so rapidly in "modern times" as to render feasible their experiment in ordered liberty.

If the Founders by education and circumstance were led to become active readers of books, an impressive number of them were also collectors of books. In one respect this should not surprise us. In the 1770s and 1780s, transportation in America was slow, and institutional repositories of knowledge rather few. Public libraries, as we know them today, did not exist. In a real sense, every man of affairs had to be his own librarian. Still, at least a few of the builders of the new nation did far more than what was minimally required for their own edification. Benjamin Franklin's personal library, for example, contained 4, 276 volumes at the time of his death in 1790. George Washington's comprised nearly 900 volumes when he died nine years later—a figure all the more remarkable since he was much less of a reader than many. Even Patrick Henry, whose only formal education was provided by his father and his uncle, and whose forte was the spoken rather than the written word, assembled a respectable 150 titles, including both ancient and modern classics. How many Americans today have libraries that could compare with these?

Early in their careers, two of the most intellectual of the Founding Fathers—John Adams and Thomas Jefferson—took extraordinary pains to create not just serviceable personal libraries but collections of superlative quality. Writing in his diary on January 30, 1768, John Adams, then a lawyer in Massachusetts, engaged in a fretful spasm of introspection. As he rushed from town to town, leading what he called a "wandering life," this young professional asked himself what it was that he was accomplishing in life:

> AM I GRASPING AT MONEY, OR SCHEMING FOR POWER? AM I PLANNING THE ILLUSTRATION OF MY FAMILY OR THE WELFARE OF MY COUNTRY? THESE ARE GREAT QUESTIONS. IN TRUTH, I AM TOSSED ABOUT SO MUCH, FROM POST TO PILLAR, THAT I HAVE NOT LEISURE AND TRANQUILITY ENOUGH, TO CONSIDER DISTINCTLY MY OWN VIEWS, OBJECTS AND FEELINGS.

Adams recorded that he was, at present, devoting himself primarily to collecting a library and was discovering that "a great deal of Thought, and Care, as well as Money, are necessary to assemble an ample and well chosen Assortment of Books."

Alas, he lamented, all this was "only a means, an Instrument. When ever I shall have completed my Library, my End will not be answered. Fame, Fortune, Power say some, are the Ends intended by a Library. The Service of God, Country, Clients, Fellow Men, say others. Which of these lie nearest my Heart?"

Adams' mood of despair passed and he went on to find abundant purpose in his life. And when he died fifty-eight years later, the library that he had conceived as an instrument of his still-unfocused ambition had grown to more than 3,000 volumes—one of the finest collections in the United States.

While Adams, in colonial Massachusetts, was busily acquiring books, a lawyer in Virginia was assiduously doing the same. Thomas Jefferson began to collect books while a law student in Williamsburg; shortly before he turned twenty-seven he had assembled a library whose worth he calculated at the not inconsiderable sum of £200. In that year (1770) he lost it all when his home went up in flames. Undaunted, he promptly set out to amass a second library, which attained the size of 1,256 volumes in just three years. By 1783, his collection had more than doubled, and all 2,640 volumes had been elaborately catalogued by Jefferson himself according to a classification scheme derived from his hero, Sir Francis Bacon. Throughout his more than eighty-three years of life, the indefatigable Virginian never stopped buying books, loaning books to friends, and advising both acquaintances and relatives on worthy books to read. While serving as ambassador to France in the mid-1780s, he devoted many a spare afternoon to rummaging through the bookstores of Paris in search of treasures, especially those relating to America. "I cannot live without books," he told John Adams in 1815. By that year Jefferson's library was probably the greatest personal collection in our country.

The luminaries of the revolutionary generation were more than readers and book collectors, however. They were also, in a sense that I have already intimated, users of books. I do not mean to suggest that these extraordinary individuals could not enjoy reading for its own sake. Long after he had ceased to have any utilitarian reason for doing so, for instance, John Adams found delight in books. In his eighty-second year, he read no fewer than forty-three of them. Jefferson, in his retirement, shared this enthusiasm and at one point confessed to having a "canine appetite for reading." Years earlier, not long before he assumed the presidency, the Virginian wrote to a friend: "To read Latin and Greek authors in their original, is a sublime luxury."

Nevertheless, what seems most noteworthy about the Founding Fathers' reading habits, at least during their active years on the public stage, was their tendency to regard books not as ornaments but as tools. Once again, John Adams provides an apt example. In his surviving library, there are more than one hundred works of eighteenth-century European political philosophy containing extensive marginal notations by Adams himself. From these sometimes mordant, often argumentative, and occasionally lengthy handwritten comments, one can at times construct a virtual line-by-line dialogue between the European author (Rousseau, Voltaire, or whomever) and the feisty New Englander who penned his responses right on the printed page. In fact, some years ago a scholar in Boston compiled these marginalia into a fascinating book entitled *John Adams and the Prophets of Progress*. It is one of the most unusual evidences we have of how the Founding Fathers reacted to books, interacted with books, and used books.

Another—and very different—illustration comes from that most worldly of the Founders, Benjamin Franklin. In the year 1784, at the ripe old age of seventy-eight, Franklin wrote a letter to the son of the Puritan minister, Cotton Mather:

> WHEN I WAS A BOY, I MET WITH A BOOK, ENTITLED "*ESSAYS TO DO GOOD*," WHICH I THINK WAS WRITTEN BY YOUR FATHER. IT HAD BEEN SO LITTLE REGARDED BY ITS FORMER POSSESSOR, THAT SEVERAL LEAVES OF IT WERE TORN OUT; BUT THE REMAINDER GAVE ME SUCH A TURN OF THINKING, AS TO HAVE AN INFLUENCE ON MY CONDUCT THROUGH LIFE; FOR I HAVE ALWAYS SET A GREATER VALUE ON THE CHARACTER OF A *DOER OF GOOD*, THAN ON ANY OTHER KIND OF REPUTATION; AND IF I HAVE BEEN, AS YOU SEEM TO THINK, A USEFUL CITIZEN, THE PUBLIC OWES THE ADVANTAGE OF IT TO THAT BOOK.

Franklin was not the only American of his era whose entire life was profoundly affected by a book. George Washington was another. In his case the book was a play, one of the most popular plays of the eighteenth century: *Cato*, written by the Englishman Joseph Addison. In it, the ancient Roman statesman Cato—wise, noble, heroic—falls on his sword at Utica rather than surrender to the conquering armies of Julius Caesar. For American audiences of the time, *Cato* was a powerful morality play, an unforgettable discourse on republican virtue and the evils of Caesarean tyranny. Not a few colonials were inspired by Addison's eloquence and fervor. Patrick Henry's immortal words "Give me liberty or give me death!" bear a noticeable resemblance to certain of Addison's verses. Nathan Hale's dying regret that he had but one life to lose for his country recalled these lines from Act IV:

> WHAT PITY IS IT
> THAT WE CAN DIE BUT ONCE TO SERVE OUR COUNTRY!

An avid theatergoer, George Washington loved this play. He quoted from it in his correspondence and ordered it to be performed in 1778 at Valley Forge; he even quoted a line from it when he decided in 1796 to retire from the presidency. There is little doubt that Roman stoicism, mediated through a British stage play written in 1713, exerted an indelible influence on America's first president. Like Franklin, Washington discovered a persona in a book.

Washington and Franklin were not alone among their contemporaries in this regard. In their often polemical, public writings, a number of the founding generation at times chose Greek or Latinate pseudonyms derived from their knowledge of ancient history. Often the pseudonym in question was intended not just to conceal the author's identity, but more importantly, to convey a political message. It was a shorthand form of argument by historical analogy. Hamilton, for instance, selected such names of "Phocion" and "Tully" when he wished to draw parallels between past and present circumstances.

More famously, in 1787 two of the most outspoken opponents of ratification of the Constitution unleashed fusillades in the press under the portentous names of "Brutus" and "Cato." Their obvious point was that the proposed new Constitution contained the seeds of Caesarean despotism. It was a point that their classically educated readers would have instantly understood.

In response to these dangerous attacks from the Anti-Federalists, three leading proponents of the Constitution penned the immortal tract called the *Federalist*. You and I know the names of its authors—James Madison, Alexander Hamilton, and John Jay. But that is not how they presented themselves in 1787. Instead, they adopted a single pen name, "Publius," after Publius Valerius Publicola, who in the sixth century B.C. helped to expel the last king of Rome and establish the Roman republic. Among his fellow citizens, Publius Valerius was acclaimed for his nobleness of character and devotion to republican principles. The authors of the *Federalist* knew that their audience would grasp the reassuring resonance of their literary allusion because of their common culture, which was formed in part by their reading of Plutarch's *Lives* and other ancient texts. The Founders' self-conscious use of politically apt, historical pseudonyms opens a small but revealing window on their mental world, a landscape adorned with shelves of well-thumbed books.

Surely the most spectacular instance, however, of the Founding Fathers' use of books was provided by that other scholarly gentleman from Virginia, James Madison. In 1784, as the Articles of Confederation increasingly manifested their fatal flaws, the youthful protégé of Thomas Jefferson launched a comprehensive study of all previous confederations in history. What were their characteristic strengths and defects? Why did they fail? How could Americans avoid a similar fate?

To facilitate his project, Madison required books, and for these he turned, appropriately, to Jefferson. In a letter dated March 16, 1784, Madison asked his friend to purchase for him "whatever may throw light on the general Constitution and droit public of the several confederacies which have existed." In a few months Jefferson was in Paris, and from France he sent back books by the score. Eventually, in the spring of 1787, after three years of determined investigation, Madison distilled his research into two memoranda and devised the Virginia Plan that framed the debate at the Constitutional Convention. Madison did not obtain all that he wanted in Philadelphia. Nevertheless, without the self-imposed historical inquiry he undertook in 1784, and the uses to which he then put it, the very structure of our republic might have been different.

In surveying the role of books in the lives of the Founding Fathers, we must not overlook still another dimension, namely that many of them were themselves creators of books, including several that have deservedly become classics. One thinks of Franklin's *Autobiography*, Jefferson's *Notes on the State of Virginia*, and Adams's *Defence of the Constitutions of Government of the United States of America*. One thinks of John Dickinson's *Letters from a Farmer in Pennsylvania* and the late-eighteenth century explosion of political pamphleteering to which I alluded earlier. And, at the pinnacle, we have the *Federalist*, America's greatest contribution to political theory—a work produced by Madison, Hamilton, and Jay in just a matter of months. Is there anyone alive today who could accomplish a similar feat of intellect in the same limited amount of time—and expect the product to be read two hundred years hence?

Sometimes, indeed, it seems that the men of 1776 and 1787 never stopped writing. Their literary output of all kinds was prodigious. Contemplate for a moment the monumental, scholarly enterprises that are now publishing in definitive form the papers of the principal Founding Fathers, including *The Papers of Alexander Hamilton*—27 volumes and now complete; *The Papers of James Madison*—29 volumes so far, and 23 more in the pipeline; *The Papers of Benjamin Franklin*—37 volumes to date, and the editors have only reached the year 1782; *The Papers of George Washington*—54 volumes (including six volumes of diaries) when I last checked the bookshelf; and *The Papers of John Adams*—so many volumes now that I have lost count. Somewhere I have read that Thomas Jefferson composed 25,000 letters during his lifetime. Whatever the figure, I do know this. When the magisterial Jefferson Papers publication project, initiated more than half a century ago by Julian Boyd, is completed, it will comprise 75 hefty volumes.

The Founding Fathers, then, were readers, collectors, users, and creators of books. A few of them went further and became founders of institutional libraries, thereby perpetuating their influence beyond the grave. The earliest to do this was Franklin. In 1731, in a club known as the Junto, the twenty-five year old Pennsylvania printer and his friends established the Library Company of Philadelphia, the first subscription library in North America. The motive behind their initiative, as well as behind the Junto itself, was partly utilitarian: a yearning on the part of Franklin and his cohorts for "mutual improvement." What is less well known, perhaps, is that the idea of forming the Junto in the first place came from a book: the very essays by Cotton Mather that Franklin credited with changing his life.

In later years, Franklin was a faithful patron of libraries. On trips to Europe, he selected books for his Library Company and had the satisfaction of seeing it serve as a reference library for the Constitutional Convention. He donated books to Harvard and Yale and to a town named after himself in Massachusetts.

He helped to develop the library of the American Philosophical Society. In these forms of benefaction he was not alone. His fellow Pennsylvanian John Dickinson donated more than 1,500 volumes to Dickinson College after it was chartered in 1783. In 1822, John Adams presented the remainder of his book collection (except for a few that he wished to retain for his "consolation" in his final days) to the town of Quincy, Massachusetts. Adams intended his books to be placed in a prospective Greek and Latin academy, which was not established until long after his death. Eventually his gift found its way to the Boston Public Library, where it survives today.

Undoubtedly, the most sublime example of this beneficent impulse comes, fittingly enough, from those two Virginia soulmates, Madison and Jefferson. In 1783, Madison attempted to persuade the Continental Congress to establish a library for its own use. With customary meticulousness, and probably with Jefferson's behind-the-scenes assistance, he even compiled a list of three hundred prospective titles. Madison's motion failed when Congress, still recovering from the costly war for independence, refused to appropriate money for such a purpose. Not until 1800, in the administration of President Adams, did the government at last create the Library of Congress.

During the next decade or so, this infant institution matured into a collection of three thousand volumes. Then, in the War of 1812, catastrophe struck. First, an American military expedition raided the capital of British-controlled Upper Canada and put its Parliament building, which happened to include the parliamentary library, to the torch. Intent on revenge, a British force of four thousand men invaded Washington, D.C., in the summer of 1814. As President Madison and his colleagues fled into the countryside, the enemy set fire to the White House and other public buildings, including the Capitol in which the Congressional Library was housed. Nearly all of its precious contents were destroyed.

Outraged at these "devastations of British Vandalism," Thomas Jefferson, by then retired and living in Monticello, promptly offered his own library of nearly sixty-five hundred books as a replacement. The United States government accepted and paid him $23,950 for what its owner proudly described as "the choicest collection of books" in the nation. By one noble stroke, the Library of Congress rose from its ashes in doubled size and acquired a breadth of holdings that foretold its emergence as a truly national library.

Even then, the aging bibliophile of the Blue Ridge was not done. As soon as he had parted with the cherished fruit of forty-five years of devoted book collecting, Jefferson, although heavily in debt, began to assemble another library in its place. By the time of his death barely a decade later, it embraced nearly a thousand volumes. More amazingly still, in these final years of his life Jefferson labored without stint to establish the University of Virginia and to design the repository of written knowledge that would be its crucial foundation. Not only did he personally select the university's first library—6,680 separate items—he also classified every single one of them and drew up the regulations for their use. His classification scheme endured for more than eighty years.

Ever the reformer, Jefferson also promoted the creation of public libraries for the general population. "I have often thought that nothing would do more extensive good at small expense," he wrote, "than the establishment of a small circulating library in every county, to consist of a few well-chosen books, to be lent to the people of the country under regulations as would secure their safe return in due time." Like Franklin and his Junto, Jefferson conceived of such libraries as instruments for the betterment of society. With access to books in local libraries, the people would be equipped to educate themselves.

I would not want you to conclude from all this that the Founding Fathers were somehow denizens of an ivory tower—"bloody-minded" intellectuals given to abstract, doctrinaire speculation and utopian schemes. They were, as I said earlier, practical men of affairs. As John Dickinson told his fellow delegates in Independence Hall during the sweltering summer of 1787, "Experience must be our only guide. Reason may mislead us." But—and the historian Douglass Adair made this point years ago—the experience which Dickinson and his confreres brought to bear upon their deliberations was not simply their personal experience, rich and instructive though that was. It was the accumulated experience of past ages derived from books. The past was real to them. It mattered. Their respect for what it could teach them was profound.

Gazing back upon these men from the perspective of two centuries, what are we to make of them now? Visiting them anew through their writings, I cannot but marvel at how different their world was from our own. They lived in a nation of barely 3,000,000 souls, of whom the vast majority were farmers. No cell phones, no Internet, no e-mail, no blogosphere bound them in instant embrace. There were no automobiles, no busses, and no shuttle jets to transport them swiftly from place to place. In the 1770s and 1780s, it took as long as six weeks for a letter to make its way from Philadelphia to London. Theirs was a less cluttered existence, theirs the last era before the onset of the Age of Specialization. In 1787, it was possible for a single individual to encompass in a personal library of a few thousand titles most of the world's important store of knowledge. Today we live in an era in which more than 170,000 separate books are published in English each year, along with literally thousands of periodicals.

The generation of the Founders differs from the generation of today in another respect. Unlike ourselves—their distant and often uncomprehending legatees—Washington, Jefferson, Hamilton, and the rest had to struggle, both physically and intellectually, to create a free and independent polity. Many of them lost their fortunes, and some their lives, in the war for liberty. Remember, too, that no other republic in history had ever survived very long or had successfully established itself over such a vast expanse of territory. It was not hyperbole for the Founders to fear that if their experiment in government-making failed, the cause of republicanism would be discredited forever. It was not hyperbole for James Wilson, a signer of the Constitution, to tell the Pennsylvania ratifying convention that "on the success of the struggle America has made for freedom will depend the exertions of the brave and enlightened of all nations." As men who had endured both war and revolution, the framers of the Constitution had to grapple with the consequences of their deeds. For better or for worse, we do not have to preoccupy ourselves with the issues that so perplexed them. Their very success has freed us for other endeavors.

Yet if the Founding Fathers were inhabitants of a world that now seems long ago and far away, they nevertheless continue to hold more than antiquarian interest for us. Like Cato for George Washington, they challenge us with the power of their example and of their searching commitment to the cause we, too, profess to hold dear. James Madison once remarked (in words now inscribed on the front of the Madison Building of the Library of Congress): "What spectacle could be more edifying or more seasonable, than that of Liberty & Learning, each leaning on the other for their mutual and surest support?" Liberty and Learning: the Founders believed earnestly that each required the other if either was to survive.

In our ever-accelerating "information age," dominated by the computer, the imagery of television, and the pervasiveness of musical sound, an age packed with fact yet increasingly devoid of cultural literacy, we can still derive inspiration from the fifty-five framers of the Constitution and their contemporaries who read, collected, used, and created books. Through books, they sought both knowledge and self-knowledge, the means by which better to live. For them books were not irrelevancies but bulwarks against barbarism and tyranny.

"I cannot live without books," said Jefferson. And neither, as a civilized people, can we.

"I am most intent at present, upon collecting a library, and I find, that a great deal of Thought, and Care, as well as Money, are necessary to assemble an ample and well chosen Assortment of Books."

Diary of John Adams
January 30, 1768

Suggestions for Further Reading

There are many points of entry into the intellectual world of the Founding Fathers, and particularly into the role that books and libraries played in shaping their lives. One of the best windows is provided by the writings of the Framers themselves, beginning with the *Autobiography* of the eldest among them, Benjamin Franklin. This American classic is accessible in many editions. Perhaps the most useful, because of its scholarly annotation and bibliography, is Leonard W. Labaree et al., eds., *The Autobiography of Benjamin Franklin*, 2nd ed. (New Haven: Yale University Press, 2003).

As noted in my essay, many of the Founders were inveterate writers. Three splendid collections of correspondence which illuminate their reading habits and mental world are: Lester J. Cappon, ed., *The Adams-Jefferson Letters* (Chapel Hill: University of North Carolina Press, 1959); John A. Schutz and Douglass Adair, eds., *The Spur of Fame: Dialogues of John Adams and Benjamin Rush, 1805-1813* (Indianapolis: Liberty Fund, 2001); and James Morton Smith, ed., *The Republic of Letters: The Correspondence between Thomas Jefferson and James Madison, 1776-1826*, 3 vols. (New York: W. W. Norton & Company, 1995). Adams's spirited "dialogue" with various contemporary European authors—in the form of his annotations of his copies of their books—can be followed in Zoltán Haraszti, ed., *John Adams and the Prophets of Progress* (Cambridge, Mass.: Harvard University Press, 1952).

The Library of America series, now distributed by Penguin Putnam Inc. of New York City, has published the selected writings of several leading statesmen of the Revolutionary War era. These tomes include: Merrill D. Peterson, ed., *Thomas Jefferson: Writings* (1984); J. A. Leo Lemay, ed., *Benjamin Franklin: Writings* (1987); John Rhodehamel, ed., *George Washington: Writings* (1997); Jack N. Rakove, ed., *James Madison: Writings* (1999); and Joanne B. Freeman, ed., *Alexander Hamilton: Writings* (2001). Each of these impressive collections holds a variety of treasures. The volume for Franklin, for instance, contains the complete text of his autobiography and *Poor Richard's Almanac.* The Jefferson volume reprints in entirety his *Notes on the State of Virginia.* For those who wish to delve still more deeply, there are the magisterial, multivolume editions of the papers of the principal Founding Fathers. Among the statesmen whose lives have been, or are still being, documented in this way are: John Adams (Harvard University Press), Benjamin Franklin (Yale University Press), Alexander Hamilton (Columbia University Press), Thomas Jefferson (Princeton University Press), James Madison (University of Chicago Press, succeeded by the University Press of Virginia), George Mason (University of North Carolina Press), Robert Morris (University of Pittsburgh Press), and George Washington (University Press of Virginia).

The Founders' love of learning, and the practical uses to which they put it, are well displayed in Bernard Bailyn, ed., *The Debate on the Constitution,* 2 vols. (New York, 1993), another contribution to the Library of America series. See also George W. Carey and James McClellan, eds., *The Federalist* (Indianapolis: Liberty Fund, 2001), an elegant scholarly edition of the classic text by Alexander Hamilton, James Madison, and John Jay; and Colleen A. Sheehan and Gary L. McDowell, eds., *Friends of the Constitution: Writings of the "Other" Federalists, 1787-1788* (Indianapolis: Liberty Fund, 1998). John Adams's three-volume *Defense of the Constitutions of Government of the United States of America* (1787) can be found in Charles Francis Adams, ed., *The Works of John Adams,* vol.

4 (Boston: Charles C. Little and James Brown, 1851), pp. 271-588, and vol. 5 (Boston: Charles C. Little and James Brown, 1851), pp. 3-220. For the anti-Federalists, who were as steeped in classical learning as their antagonists, see Herbert J. Storing, ed., *The Complete Anti-Federalist*, 7 vols. (Chicago and London: University of Chicago Press, 1981).

A magnificent compilation of "extracts from all the leading works of political theory, history, law, and constitutional argument on which the Framers and their contemporaries drew and which they themselves produced" is Philip B. Kurland and Ralph Lerner, eds., *The Founders' Constitution*, 5 vols. (Indianapolis: Liberty Fund, 2000). The entire set is accessible online at http://press-pubs.uichicago.edu/founders/. It includes literally hundreds of primary source documents.

Joseph Addison's stage play *Cato* (1713), which did so much to inform the moral sensibility of eighteenth century Americans, has recently come back into print in a fine, scholarly edition prepared by Christine Dunn Henderson and Mark E. Yellin: Joseph Addison, *Cato: A Tragedy and Selected Essays* (Indianapolis: Liberty Fund, 2004).

The education, reading habits, and intellectual interests of the Founding Fathers are explored in varying detail in a host of modern biographies, too numerous to cite here but easily locatable in libraries. One convenient entrée into the subject is M. E. Bradford, *Founding Fathers: Brief Lives of the Framers of the United States Constitution*, 2nd ed., revised (Lawrence: University Press of Kansas, 1994), a collection of fifty-five pithy essays, each with a helpful bibliography. Similar in scope and design is Joseph C. Norton, *Shapers of the Great Debate at the Constitutional Convention of 1787: A Biographical Dictionary* (Westport, Ct.: Greenwood Press, 2006), which also has fifty-five entries—one (like Bradford's volume) for each participant in the Constitutional Convention. Not everyone, of course, who was influential in American politics in 1787 attended the convention in Philadelphia. John Adams (ambassador to Great Britain) and Thomas Jefferson (ambassador to France) were absent, as were such estimable figures as Patrick Henry and John Jay. Still, the Bradford and Norton volumes cover a large expanse of biographical territory. From these sources much can be gleaned about the importance of learning to the men who made the nation.

Apart from biographies (a few of which will be mentioned below), a number of specialized studies have focused on the role of books and libraries in the intellectual formation of America's founding generation. Three excellent surveys of this subject are: 1) Forrest McDonald, "A Founding Father's Library," *Literature of Liberty* 1 (January/March 1978): 4-15; 2) Jack P. Greene, *The Intellectual Heritage of the Constitutional Era: The Delegates' Library* (Philadelphia: Library Company of Philadelphia, 1986); and 3) Robert A. Rutland, *"Well-Acquainted with Books": The Founding Framers of 1787* (Washington, D.C.: Library of Congress, 1987).

For Benjamin Franklin, see Edwin Wolf II, "Franklin and His Friends Choose Their Books," *Pennsylvania Magazine of History and Biography* 80 (January 1956): 11-36; Edwin Wolf II, "The Reconstruction of Benjamin Franklin's Library: An Unorthodox Jigsaw Puzzle," *Papers of the Bibliographical Society of America* 56 (First Quarter, 1962): 1-16; and Edwin Wolf II, "Franklin's Library," in J. A. Leo Lemay, ed., *Reappraising Benjamin Franklin: A Bicentennial Perspective* (Newark, Del.: University of Delaware Press, 1993), pp. 319-31. A recent monograph which carefully examines Franklin's educational development, and the influence of books thereon, is Douglas Anderson, *The Radical Enlightenments of Benjamin Franklin* (Baltimore: Johns Hopkins University Press, 1997). Edwin S. Gaustad's just-published brief biography, *Benjamin Franklin* (Oxford and New York: Oxford

University Press, 2006) is a luminous introduction to the intellectual interests and accomplishments of this most versatile of the Founding Fathers.

For the influence of *Cato* upon George Washington, see Forrest McDonald, "Washington, Cato, and Honor: A Model for Revolutionary Leadership," in Daniel J. Elazar and Ellis Katz, eds., *American Models of Revolutionary Leadership: George Washington and Other Founders* (Lanham, Md.: University Press of America, 1992), pp. 43-58. McDonald's introduction to the recent (2004) edition of *Cato*, cited above, also discusses the impact of this immensely popular play upon Washington and others. Gary L. Gregg II and Matthew Spaulding, eds., *Patriot Sage: George Washington and the American Political Tradition* (Wilmington, Del.: ISI Books, 1999) is an assemblage of a dozen scholarly essays that shed light upon Washington's education, worldview, and much else. Recently Washington's religious ideas and ambiguous faith have received fresh scholarly scrutiny, with conflicting results. See Michael Novak and Jana Novak, *Washington's God: Religion, Liberty, and the Faith of Our Country* (New York: Basic Books, 2006) and Peter Henriques, *Realistic Visionary: A Portrait of George Washington* (Charlottesville: University of Virginia Press, 2006).

Thomas Jefferson's passionate love of books and libraries has long been noted by his biographers. See, for example, Dumas Malone, *Jefferson and His Time*, 6 vols. (Boston: Little, Brown and Company, 1948-1981) and Merrill D. Peterson, *Thomas Jefferson and the New Nation* (New York: Oxford University Press, 1970). Highly informative is Charles B. Sanford, *Thomas Jefferson and His Library: A Study of His Literary Interests and of the Religious Attitudes Revealed by Relevant Titles in His Library* (Hamden, Ct.: Anchor Books, 1977). A comprehensive, annotated catalogue of Jefferson's library as of 1815—the collection which became the nucleus of the restored Library of Congress—is E. Millicent Sowerby, comp., *Catalogue of the Library of Thomas Jefferson*, 5 vols. (Washington, D.C.:

Library of Congress, 1952-1959), reprinted by the University Press of Virginia in 1983. Excellent essays on Jefferson's library, his interest in the classics, and related topics can be found in Merrill D. Peterson, ed., *Thomas Jefferson: A Reference Biography* (New York: Charles Scribner's Sons, 1986).

For insight into that other Virginia bibliophile, James Madison, see Robert A. Rutland, "Madison's Bookish Habits," *Quarterly Journal of the Library of Congress* 37 (Spring 1980): 176-91. Like Jefferson, Madison was an ardent consumer and cataloguer of books. In 1783, in response to a resolution by the Continental Congress, he meticulously prepared "a list of books proper for the use of Congress," which he hoped that it would purchase for ready reference. His compilation embraced more than three hundred entries. Although Congress, suffering from severe financial constraints, rejected his recommendation, his report nevertheless reflected what this most bookish of the Founders deemed appropriate reading matter for the men at the helm of the nation. His catalogue is printed in Robert A. Rutland's *"Well Acquainted with Books"* (cited earlier) and in William L. Hutchinson and William M. E. Rachal, eds., *The Papers of James Madison*, vol. 6 (Chicago and London: University of Chicago Press, 1969), pp. 62-115.

For Alexander Hamilton's exposure to books, and their influence upon his career, Forrest McDonald's *Alexander Hamilton: A Biography* (New York: W. W. Norton & Company, 1979) is instructive, as is Ron Chernow's *Alexander Hamilton* (New York: Penguin Press, 2004).

The larger intellectual world of the Founders has been the subject of intense, and even profound, scholarly investigation in recent decades. Not to be missed are Bernard Bailyn's classic, *The Ideological Origins of the American Revolution* (Cambridge, Mass.: Harvard University Press, 1967), and two sparkling sets of Bailyn's essays: *Faces of Revolution: Personalities and Themes in the Struggle for*

American Independence (New York: Alfred A. Knopf, 1990) and *To Begin the World Anew: The Genius and Ambiguities of the American Founders* (New York: Alfred A. Knopf, 2003). Nor should anyone overlook Forrest McDonald's learned and lively *Novus Ordo Seclorum: The Intellectual Origins of the Constitution* (Lawrence: University Press of Kansas, 1985). McDonald's 1987 Jefferson Lecture at the National Endowment for the Humanities was entitled "The Intellectual World of the Founding Fathers." He has reprinted it in his collection of essays, *Requiem: Variations on Eighteenth Century Themes* (Lawrence: University Press of Kansas, 1988), coauthored with his wife Ellen Shapiro McDonald.

Also well worth reading are the penetrating essays gathered in Trevor Colbourn, ed., *Fame and the Founding Fathers: Essays by Douglass Adair* (Indianapolis: Liberty Fund, 1998). Forty years later, Adair's insights into the mindset and motivation of the Framers continue to influence scholars. Trevor Colbourn's own book, *The Lamp of Experience: Whig History and the Intellectual Origins of the American Revolution* (Chapel Hill: University of North Carolina Press, 1965) has also stood the test of time; it is now available in a Liberty Fund edition (Indianapolis, 1998).

For the impact of the Enlightenment upon the Founders, two models of scholarship leap to mind: Henry F. May, *The Enlightenment in America* (New York: Oxford University Press, 1976) and I. Bernhard Cohen, *Science and the Founding Fathers: Science in the Political Thought of Jefferson, Franklin, Adams, and Madison* (New York: W. W. Norton & Company, 1995).

The influence of the classics on the Revolutionary War generation has often been noted by historians and biographers. Two relatively recent works which provocatively reexamine this subject are: 1) Meyer Reinhold, *Classica Americana: The Greek and Roman Heritage in the United States* (Detroit: Wayne State University Press, 1984), and 2) Carl J. Richard, *The Founders and the*

Classics: Greece, Rome, and the American Enlightenment (Cambridge, Mass.: Harvard University Press, 1994). See also E. Christian Kopff, *The Devil Knows Latin* (Wilmington, Del.: ISI Books, 1999), pp. 43-54; Tracy Lee Simmons, *Climbing Parnassus: A New Apologia for Greek and Latin* (Wilmington, Del.: ISI Books, 2002), pp. 198-210; and Albert Furtwangler's stimulating volume of essays, *American Silhouettes: Rhetorical Identities of the Founders* (New Haven and London: Yale University Press, 1987), including one entitled "Cato at Valley Forge."

For a refreshingly panoramic and highly readable historical account of the intellectual and spiritual patrimony of the Founders—from ancient Israel, Greece, and Rome to Montesquieu, Burke, and Hume—see Russell Kirk, *The Roots of American Order*, 4th edition (Wilmington, Del.: ISI Books, 2004). It is a work intended for a creature that scholars sometimes lose sight of, namely, the intellectually oriented general reader.

No bibliographical essay on "Books and the Founding Fathers" would be complete without mention of the magnificent Library of Congress, which Jefferson and Madison did so much to create and preserve. It is one of the greatest legacies of the founding generation. Readers interested in the Library's origins and history should consult John Y. Cole, *For Congress and the Nation: A Chronological History of the Library of Congress* (Washington, D.C.: Library of Congress, 1979) and James Conaway, *America's Library: The Story of the Library of Congress, 1800-2000* (New Haven: Yale University Press, 2000).

Finally, anyone seeking seriously to enter the "lost world" of Thomas Jefferson and his contemporaries should become familiar with the ongoing publishing program of the Liberty Fund in Indianapolis. In the past generation the Fund has published a number of influential, long out-of-print works on eighteenth-century American history, as well as exemplary, scholarly collections of documents on the Revolution, the Constitution, and the political debates of the founding era. The current Liberty Fund catalogue lists more than two dozen such titles, all in handsome, yet affordable editions. Several have been cited above. The Liberty Fund also maintains at its website (www.libertyfund.org) a massive Online Library of Liberty, consisting of the complete texts of more than 1,400 books, both ancient and modern, which "have contributed to an understanding of the nature of individual liberty, limited and constitutional government, and the free market." This ever-growing electronic treasure trove currently includes the full texts of thirty-seven books and essays pertaining to the American Revolution and Constitution.

At this point I shall resist the temptation to convert a "select bibliography" into an *omnium gatherum* beyond the needs of most readers. Most of the sources already cited, of course, have bibliographies of their own. My aim here is to open a window onto the mental world of a remarkable galaxy of American statesmen and to provide a pathway for further investigation. I hope that at least a few readers will decide to follow that path—perhaps for a considerable distance. If you do, you will find the Founders to be worthy and agreeable companions in the pursuit of liberty and learning.

– George H. Nash

"I conceive that a knowledge of books is the basis on which all other knowledge rests."

George Washington

Benjamin Franklin's Notes on the Utility of his Initial Book Club and the Public Library that It Became

From the autobiography of Benjamin Franklin (Part II)
1784

At the time I establish'd my self in Pensylvania, there was not a good Bookseller's Shop in any of the Colonies to the Southward of Boston. In New-York and Philadelphia the Printers were indeed Stationers, they sold only Paper, &c., Almanacks, Ballads, and a few common School Books. Those who lov'd Reading were oblig'd to send for their Books from England. The Members of the Junto had each a few. We had left the Alehouse where we first met, and hired a Room to hold our Club in. I propos'd that we should all of us bring our Books to that Room, where they would not only be ready to consult in our Conferences, but become a common Benefit, each of us being at Liberty to borrow such as he wish'd to read at home. This was accordingly done, and for some time contented us. Finding the Advantage of this little Collection, I propos'd to render the Benefit from Books more common by commencing a Public Subscription Library. I drew a Sketch of the Plan and Rules that would be necessary, and got a skilful Conveyancer, Mr. Charles Brockden to put the whole in Form of Articles of Agreement to be subscribed; by which each Subscriber engag'd to pay a certain Sum down for the first Purchase of Books and an annual Contribution for encreasing them. So few were the Readers at that time in Philadelphia, and the Majority of us so poor, that I was not able with great Industry to find more than Fifty Persons, mostly young Tradesmen, willing to pay down for this purpose Forty shillings each, and Ten Shillings per Annum. On this little Fund we began. The books were imported. The Library was open one Day in the Week for lending them to the Subscribers, on their Promisory Notes to pay Double the Value if not duly returned. The Institution soon manifested its Utility, was imitated by other Towns and in other Provinces, the Librarys were augmented by Donations, Reading became fashionable, and our People having no publick Amusements to divert their Attention from Study became better acquainted with Books, and in a few Years were observ'd by Strangers to be better instructed and more intelligent than People of the same Rank generally are in other Countries. . . .

This Library afforded me the means of Improvement by constant Study, for which I set apart an Hour or two each Day; and thus repair'd in some Degree the loss of the Learned Education my Father once intended for me. Reading was the only Amusement I allow'd my self. I spent no time in Taverns, Games, or Frolicks of any kind. And my Industry in my Business continu'd as indefatigable as it was necessary.

Thoughts on Collecting a Library

From the diary of John Adams
January 30, 1768

To what Object, are my Views directed? What is the End and Purpose of my Studies, Journeys, Labours of all Kinds of Body and Mind, of Tongue and Pen? Am I grasping at Money, or Scheming for Power? Am I planning the Illustration of my Family or the Welfare of my Country? These are great Questions. In Truth, I am tossed about so much, from Post to Pillar, that I have not Leisure and Tranquillity enough, to consider distinctly my own Views, Objects and Feelings.—I am mostly intent at present, upon collecting a Library, and I find, that a great deal of Thought, and Care, as well as Money, are necessary to assemble an ample and well chosen Assortment of Books.—But when this is done, it is only a means, an Instrument. When ever I shall have compleated my Library, my End will not be answered. Fame, Fortune, Power say some, are the Ends intended by a Library. The Service of God, Country, Clients, Fellow Men, say others. Which of these lie nearest my Heart? Self Love but serves the virtuous Mind to wake as the small Pebble stirs the Peacefull Lake, The Center Moved, a Circle straight succeeds, another still and still another spreads. Friend, Parent, Neighbour, first it does embrace, our Country next and next all human Race.

I am certain however, that the Course I pursue will neither lead me to Fame, Fortune, Power Nor to the Service of my Friends, Clients or Country. What Plan of Reading or Reflection, or Business can be pursued by a Man, who is now at Pownalborough, then at Marthas Vineyard, next at Boston, then at Taunton, presently at Barnstable, then at Concord, now at Salem, then at Cambridge, and afterwards at Worcester. Now at Sessions, then at Pleas, now in Admiralty, now at Superiour Court, then in the Gallery of the House. What a Dissipation must this be? Is it possible to pursue a regular Train of Thinking in this desultory Life?—By no means.—It is a Life of *Here and every where*, to use the Expression, that is applied to Othello, by Desdemona's Father. Here and there and every where, a rambling, roving, vagrant, vagabond Life. A wandering Life. . . .

Thomas Jefferson's offer to Re-establish the Library of Congress

To Samuel H. Smith
Monticello, September 21, 1814

DEAR SIR,--I learn from the newspapers that the Vandalism of our enemy has triumphed at Washington over science as well as the arts, by the destruction of the public library with the noble edifice in which it was deposited. Of this transaction, as of that of Copenhagen, the world will entertain but one sentiment. They will see a nation suddenly withdrawn from a great war, full armed and full handed, taking advantage of another whom they had recently forced into it, unarmed, and unprepared, to indulge themselves in acts of barbarism which do not belong to a civilized age. When Van Ghent destroyed their shipping at Chatham, and De Ruyter rode triumphantly up the Thames, he might in like manner, by the acknowledgment of their own historians, have forced all their ships up to London bridge, and there have burnt them, the tower, and city, had these examples been then set. London, when thus menaced, was near a thousand years old, Washington is but in its teens.

I presume it will be among the early objects of Congress to re-commence their collection. This will be difficult while the war continues, and intercourse with Europe is attended with so much risk. You know my collection, its condition and extent. I have been fifty years making it, and have spared no pains, opportunity or expense, to make it what it is. While residing in Paris, I devoted every afternoon

I was disengaged, for a summer or two, in examining all the principal bookstores, turning over every book with my own hand, and putting by everything which related to America, and indeed whatever was rare and valuable in every science. Besides this, I had standing orders during the whole time I was in Europe, on its principal book-marts, particularly Amsterdam, Frankfort, Madrid and London, for such works relating to America as could not be found in Paris. So that in that department particularly, such a collection was made as probably can never again be effected, because it is hardly probable that the same opportunities, the same time, industry, perseverance and expense, with some knowledge of the bibliography of the subject, would again happen to be in concurrence. During the same period, and after my return to America, I was led to procure, also, whatever related to the duties of those in the high concerns of the nation. So that the collection, which I suppose is of between nine and ten thousand volumes, while it includes what is chiefly valuable in science and literature generally, extends more particularly to whatever belongs to the American statesman. In the diplomatic and parliamentary branches, it is particularly full. It is long since I have been sensible it ought not to continue private property, and had provided that at my death, Congress should have the refusal of it at their own price. But the loss they have now incurred, makes the present the proper moment for their accommodation, without regard to the small remnant of time and the barren use of my enjoying it. I ask of your friendship, therefore, to make for me the tender of it to the library committee of Congress, not knowing myself of whom the committee consists. I enclose you the catalogue, which will enable them to judge of its contents. Nearly the whole are well bound, abundance of them elegantly, and of the choicest editions existing. They may be valued by persons named by themselves, and the payment made convenient to the public. It may be, for instance, in such annual instalments as the law of Congress has left at their disposal, or in stock of any of their late loans, or of any loan they may institute at this session, so as to spare the present calls of our country, and await its days of peace and prosperity. They may enter, nevertheless, into immediate use of it, as eighteen or twenty wagons would place it in Washington in a single trip of a fortnight. I should be willing indeed, to retain a few of the books, to amuse the time I have yet to pass, which might be valued with the rest, but not included in the sum of valuation until they should be restored at my death, which I would carefully provide for, so that the whole library as it stands in the catalogue at this moment should be theirs without any garbling. Those I should like to retain would be chiefly classical and mathematical. Some few in other branches, and particularly one of the five encyclopedias in the catalogue. But this, if not acceptable, would not be urged. I must add, that I have not revised the library since I came home to live, so that it is probable some of the books may be missing, except in the chapters of Law and Divinity, which have been revised and stand exactly as in the catalogue. The return of the catalogue will of course be needed, whether the tender be accepted or not. I do not know that it contains any branch of science which Congress would wish to exclude from their collection; there is, in fact, no subject to which a member of Congress may not have occasion to refer. But such a wish would not correspond with my views of preventing its dismemberment. My desire is either to place it in their hands entire, or to preserve it so here. I am engaged in making an alphabetical index of the author's names, to be annexed to the catalogue, which I will forward to you as soon as completed. Any agreement you shall be so good as to take the trouble of entering into with the committee, I hereby confirm. Accept the assurance of my great esteem and respect.

"Knowledge will forever govern ignorance: and a people who mean to be their own governours, must arm themselves with the power which knowledge gives."

James Madison to W.T. Barry
August 4, 1822

Thomas Jefferson, on the Last Shipment of Books to the Newly Re-established Library of Congress

Excerpt from a letter to Samuel H. Smith
Monticello, May 8, 1815

Dear Sir,

Our 10th and last wagon load of books goes off to-day. This closes the transaction here, and I cannot permit it to close without returning my thanks to you who began it. This I sincerely do for the trouble you have taken in it. When I first proposed to you to make the overture to the library committee, I thought that the only trouble you would have had, that they would have said yea, or nay directly, have appointed values, and spared you all further intermediation: and I saw with great regret this agency afterward, added to the heavy labors of your office. It is done however, and an interesting treasure is added to your city, now become the depository of unquestionably the choicest collection of books in the US and I hope it will not be without some general effect on the literature of our country.

"What spectacle can be more edifying or more seasonable, than that of liberty and learning, each leaning on the other for their mutual and surest support?"

James Madison
1822

Thomas Jefferson on his Love of Books

Excerpt from a letter to John Adams
June 10, 1815

Mr. Ticknor is particularly the best biblograph I have met with, and very kindly and opportunely offered me the means of reprocuring some part of the literary treasures which I have ceded to Congress to replace the devastations of British Vandalism at Washington. I cannot live without books; but fewer will suffice where amusement, and not use, is the only future object. I am about sending him a catalogue to which less than his critical knolege of books would hardly be adequate.

"Books constitute capital. A library book lasts as long as a house, for hundreds of years. It is not, then, an article of mere consumption, but fairly of capital; and often is the case of professional men, setting out in life, it is their only capital."

Thomas Jefferson
1821

Isaac Jefferson, On Thomas Jefferson the Writer, Book-Reader, and Teacher

An excerpt from "Memoirs of a Monticello Slave"
1847

Old master was never seen to come out before breakfast—about 8 o'clock. If it was warm weather he would'nt ride out till evening; studied upstairs till bell ring for dinner. When writing he had a copying machine: while he was a writin he would'nt suffer nobody to come in his room: had a dumb waiter: when he wanted anything he had nothing to do but turn a crank & the dumb-waiter would bring him water or fruit on a plate or anything he wanted. Old master had abundance of books: sometimes would have twenty of them down on the floor at once: read first one, then tother. Isaac has often wondered how old master came to have such a mighty head: read to many of them books: & when they go to him to ax him anything, he go right straight to the book & tell you all about it. He talked French & Italian.

"My repugnance to the writing table becomes daily and hourly more deadly and insurmountable. In place of this has come on a canine appetite for reading. And I indulge it, because I see in it a relief against the taedium senectutis; a lamp to lighten my path through the dreary wilderness of time before me, whose bourne I see not. Losing daily all interest in the things around us, something else is necessary to fill the void. With me it is reading, which occupies the mind without the labor of producing ideas from my own stock."

Thomas Jefferson to John Adams
May 17, 1818

James Madison's Praise for Kentucky's Plan for a General System of Education

To William T. Barry

August 4, 1822

Dr Sir,

I recd. Some days ago your letter of June 30, and the printed Circular to which it refers.

The liberal appropriations made by the Legislature of Kentucky for a general system of Education cannot be too much applauded. A popular Government, without popular information, or the means of acquiring it, is but a Prologue to a Farce or a Tragedy; or, perhaps both. Knowledge will forever govern ignorance: And a people who mean to be their own Governors, must arm themselves with the power which knowledge gives.

I have always felt a more than ordinary interest in the destinies of Kentucky. . . . Its rapid growth & signal prosperity in this character have afforded me much pleasure; which is not a little enhanced by the enlightened patriotism which is now providing for the State a Plan of Education embracing every class of Citizens, and every grade & department of Knowledge. No error is more certain than the one proceeding from a hasty & superficial view of the subject: that the people at large have no interest in the establishment of Academies, Colleges, and Universities, where a few only, and those not of the poorer classes can obtain for their sons the advantages of superior education. It is thought to be unjust that all should be taxed for the benefit of a part, and that too the part least needing it.

If provision were not made at the same time for every part, the objection would be a natural one. But, besides the consideration when the higher Seminaries belong to a plan of general education, that it is better for the poorer classes to have the aid of the richer by a general tax on property, than that every parent should provide at his own expence for the education of his children, it is certain that every Class is interested in establishments which give to the human mind its highest improvements, and to every Country its truest and most durable celebrity.

Learned Institutions ought be favorite objects with every free people. They throw that light over the public mind which is the best security against crafty & dangerous encroachments on the public liberty. They are the nurseries of skilful Teachers for the schools distributed throughout the Community. They are themselves schools for the particular talents required for some of the Public Trusts, on the able execution of which the welfare of the people depends. They multiply the educated individuals from among whom the people may elect a due portion of their public Agents of every description; more especially of those who are to frame the laws; by the perspicuity, the consistency, and the stability, as well as by the just & equal spirit of which the great social purposes are to be answered.

Without such Institutions, the more costly of which can scarcely be provided by individual means, none but the few whose wealth enables them to support their sons abroad can give them the fullest education; and in proportion as this is done, the influence is monopolized which superior information every where possesses. At cheaper & nearer seats of Learning parents with slender incomes may place their sons in a course of education putting them on a level with the sons of the Richest. Whilst those who are without property, or with but little, must be peculiarly interested in a System which unites with the more Learned Institutions, a provision for diffusing through the entire Society the education needed for the common purposes of life. A system comprising the Learned Institutions may be still further recommended to the more indigent class of Citizens by such an arrangement as was reported to the General Assembly of Virginia, in the year 1779, by a Committee appointed to revise laws in order to adapt them to the genius of Republican Government. It made part of a "Bill for the more general diffusion of knowledge" that wherever a youth was ascertained to possess talents meriting an education which his parents could not afford, he should be carried forward at the public expence, from seminary to seminary, to the completion of his studies at the highest.

But why should it be necessary in this case, to distinguish the Society into classes according to their property? When it is considered that the establishment and endowment of Academies, Colleges, and Universities are a provision, not merely for the existing generation, but for succeeding ones also; that in Governments like ours a constant rotation of property results from the free scope to industry and from the laws of inheritance, and when it is considered moreover, how much of the exertions and privations of all are meant not for themselves, but for their posterity, there can be little ground for objections from any class, to plans of which every class must have its turn of benefits. . . .

Throughout the Civilized World, nations are courting the praise of fostering Science and the useful Arts, and are opening their eyes to the principles and the blessings of Representative Government. The American people owe it to themselves, and to the cause of free Government, to prove by their establishments for the advancement and diffusion of Knowledge, that their political Institutions, which are attracting observation from every quarter, and are respected as Models, by the new-born States in our own Hemisphere, are as favorable to the intellectual and moral improvement of Man as they are conformable to his individual & social Rights. What spectacle can be more edifying or more seasonable, than that of Liberty & Learning, each leaning on the other for their mutual & surest support?

The Committee, of which your name is the first, have taken a very judicious course in endeavouring to avail Kentucky of the experience of elder States, in modifying her Schools. . . .

I know not that I can offer on the occasion any suggestions not likely to occur to the Committee. Were I to hazard one, it would be in favour of adding to Reading, Writing, & Arithmetic, to which the instruction of the poor, is commonly limited, some knowledge of Geography; such as can easily be conveyed by a Globe & Maps, and a concise Geographical Grammar. And how easily & quickly might a general idea even, be conveyed of the Solar System, by the aid of a Planatarium of the Cheapest construction. No information seems better calculated to expand the mind and gratify curiosity than what would thus be imparted. This is expecially the case, with what relates to the Globe we inhabit, the Nations among which it is divided, and the characters and customs which distinguish them. An acquaintance with foreign Countries in this mode, has a kindred effect with that of seeing them as travelers, which never fails, in uncorrupted minds, to weaken local prejudices, and enlarge the sphere of benevolent feelings. A knowledge of the Globe & its various inhabitants, however slight, might moreover, create a taste for Books of Travels and Voyages; out of which might grow a general taste for History, an inexhaustible fund of entertainment & instruction. Any reading not of a vicious species must be a good substitute for the amusements too apt to fill up the leisure of the labouring classes.

I feel myself much obliged Sir by your expressions of personal kindness, and pray you to accept a return of my good wishes, with assurances of my great esteem & respect.

www.mcconnellcenter.org

ABOUT THE McCONNELL CENTER

The McConnell Center was established in 1991 by U.S. Senator Mitch McConnell and the University of Louisville. McConnell, a 1964 graduate of the University, founded the center based on his belief that "Kentucky's future depends on inspiring talented, motivated leaders."

The McConnell Center is dedicated to providing a non-partisan, well-rounded education that encourages top undergraduates to become valued citizens and future leaders of the Commonwealth and the nation. The Center also facilitates public discussion on the major challenges of our time while encouraging an understanding of our shared past.

McConnell Scholarships for Young Leaders

The McConnell Center is home to one of the most competitive and prestigious scholarship programs in Kentucky. Each year, the Center's scholarship competition attracts outstanding high school seniors from around the Commonwealth. Students apply on-line to the University of Louisville and the McConnell Center, and finalists take part in a two-day interview process. Ten students are then selected as the McConnell Scholars and awarded a four-year scholarship to the University of Louisville.

McConnell Scholars receive tuition scholarships to the University of Louisville, have the chance to meet today's most influential leaders, interact with experts in a variety of fields from across the nation, intern in fields of their choice, and travel the world. In its first fifteen years, the Center has given more than one hundred students nearly $2 million in scholarship money, mentored them to compete for elite national scholarships for graduate school, and helped them travel the world from the Highlands of Scotland to the most rural village of China.

Graduates of the program have gone on to further study at such institutions as Harvard Law School, Johns Hopkins University, Oxford University, and Cambridge University in England. Though McConnell Scholars have a diversity of professional interests and academic majors, some students have decided to enter politics and government service and have served in top positions from the Governor's Mansion to the White House.

If you are an outstanding young student leader, apply for the McConnell Scholars Program at the University of Louisville during the fall of your senior year of high school. Who can tell where it will take you?

Leadership, Government, and History Institutes for Future Leaders

The McConnell Center annually sponsors weekend seminars and institutes for high school students that feature top experts in fields related to government and leadership.

Professional Development for Teachers

The McConnell Center believes that America's future depends on educating our young people about our history and our political institutions. Realizing that all of us might not be scientists or mathematicians, but we will all be citizens, the Center is dedicated to helping teachers impact the future by teaching our past. The Center regularly runs professional development programs for teachers in a variety of formats, from small seminars to week-long institutes.

Public Education Programs

Every year the McConnell Center hosts educational programs for the University and general public. The Center's Distinguished Lecture Series has brought more than 30 of today's most important leaders to Louisville, including Secretaries of State Colin Powell, Madeleine Albright, and Condoleezza Rice. The Center also regularly hosts some of today's most interesting authors and experts from a variety of fields. All programs are open to the public and are usually free of charge.

Publications and Scholarship

The McConnell Center believes in the continuing importance of the printed word and the efficacy of first-rate academic scholarship. To enhance our dialogue on perennial topics, as well as the concerns of the moment, the Center has published a variety of pamphlets, small books, and studies on topics from the history of the Senate to the relevance of the Electoral College. Most of these are available in small quantities for educational purposes. The Center also supports the work of a variety of academic leaders doing important research on topics related to American history, politics, and leadership.

Find out more at www.mcconnellcenter.org